Motivation

Boost Your Motivation with Powerful Mindfulness Techniques and Be Unstoppable

By James Adler

Copyright ©2016

All rights reserved. No part of this publication may be reproduced, stored in a retrieval system, or transmitted, in any form or by any means, electronic, mechanical, photocopying, recording or otherwise without the prior written permission of the author and the publishers.

The scanning, uploading, and distribution of this book via the Internet, or via any other means, without the permission of the author is illegal and punishable by law. Please purchase only authorized electronic editions, and do not participate in or encourage electronic piracy of copyrighted materials.

All information in this book has been carefully researched and checked for factual accuracy. However, the author and publishers make no warranty, expressed or implied, that the information contained herein is appropriate for every individual, situation or purpose, and assume no responsibility for errors or omission. The reader assumes the risk and full responsibility for all actions, and the author will not be held liable for any loss or damage, whether consequential, incidental, and special or otherwise, that may result from the information presented in this publication.

The book is not intended to provide medical advice or to take the place of medical advice and treatment from your personal physician. Readers are advised to consult their own doctors or other qualified mental health professionals regarding the treatment of medical conditions. The author shall not be held liable or responsible for any misunderstanding or misuse of the information contained in this book. The information is not intended to diagnose, treat or cure any disease.

Mindfulness Techniques that Really Work to Propel You on Your Journey

Chapter One...6
Introduction: What is Motivation?
Chapter Two...11
Mindfulness for Unlimited Motivation
Chapter Three...28
Mindful Motivation Techniques for Personal Success
Chapter Four...41
How to Deal with Adversity in a Mindful, Proactive Way

Chapter One
Introduction: What is Motivation?

We all have goals in life. You are reading this book because you are looking for inspiration and techniques that will increase your motivation and bring you closer to your goals. Maybe you want to get in shape. Maybe you want to excel in your career. Maybe you want to be an outstanding musician or artist, or pursue some other outlet for your creativity. In general, any time we want something, we are trying to get from where we are right now, to where we would like to be—from *Point A* to *Point B*. And to move along the path between these two points, we need fuel for the journey.

Motivation is the fuel that drives you towards your goals. It comes from desire, and from a vision of your ideal future. It is the emotional energy that pushes you along your journey to actualizing your dreams.

Like any other kind of energy, motivation can be strong or weak, concentrated or scattered. If your motivation is weak or vague, you will not make much progress. You will feel dissatisfied and wonder why you feel so much inner resistance to achieving your goals. You may even have a sense of low physical and psychological energy. It will seem that something is *missing*.

With strong motivation, you will feel energetic, focused, and happy. You'll have a strong sense of direction and purpose, as well as a feeling that you're *moving towards your ideal future* at a pretty good clip. When obstacles get in your way, you will cheerfully find ways to remove them or steer around them. Much of the time, it will even seem as if your path is clearing itself before you, to make way for you on your journey.

It's an obvious choice: if you had to pick strong or weak motivation, wouldn't strong motivation win hands down? I know I always prefer that feeling of energy and purpose that comes with strong motivation over listlessness, boredom, and hesitation.

One of the important things to understand about motivation is the difference between *extrinsic* and *intrinsic* motivation. *Extrinsic motivation* comes from outside you. It could come from pressure at work, or from your family or friends. It could be that somebody planted an idea in your head that you should do this or that. Whatever the case, the problem with extrinsic motivation is that it doesn't come from what you really want. That's why it can't really give you the drive and force that you need to accomplish your goals—and even if you do accomplish them, you won't feel very satisfied for very long, because you didn't *really* want to.

Intrinsic motivation, on the other hand, comes from within you. When you *really want* something, and your passion moves you to achieve it—that's intrinsic motivation. To have this kind of motivation, you need clarity about yourself and your desires and goals, and you need to have the confidence that comes from knowing that you are good enough to have big dreams. That comes from self-knowledge and self-love—and that's where meditation comes in.

Steps for this chapter

- Stop and think about the various things you are trying to do in your life, and ask yourself whether your motivation is intrinsic or extrinsic. I find it helpful to write these things down—something about putting my thoughts into the written word brings the big picture into sharper focus.

- Consider the qualities associated with strong and weak motivation, respectively. Look at your own life and situation and see which qualities are at work. Do you feel inertia, weariness, low mood levels, distraction, or lack of clarity? Or do you have focus, energy, drive, and cheerfulness?

At this point, just *look* at your life and yourself; don't worry about trying to change anything just yet. The willingness to take a look at yourself with an honest and unflinching eye is a powerful and transformative mindfulness practice by itself.

The purpose of this is not to be overly critical and to beat yourself up over your shortcomings. We are not trying to evaluate anything as "good" or "bad;" we are just opening a space for self-honesty and coming into contact with the reality of our situation. In fact, your willingness to build an honest relationship with yourself is a good sign, and a good reason for you to rejoice and feel optimistic!

My Notes:

Chapter Two
Mindfulness for Unlimited Motivation

If you're interested in holistic living, you're probably already familiar with mindfulness. After all, it's all the rage right now, and for good reason. The rise of the mindfulness revolution is fueled by tons of scientific research that shows mindfulness's many benefits, has been widely reported in the media—both traditional and social—and is spearheaded by influential figures like meditation expert Jon Kabat-Zinn and psychologist Daniel Goleman.

But at this point, you might be asking yourself what

mindfulness meditation has to do with motivation. After all, doesn't meditation have to do with just resting and being content? And if motivation is anything, it's the drive to achieve or gain something. Won't all that contentment get in the way of the motivation to achieve and change? It seems that meditation and motivation should be opposites.

But meditation is about more than contentment and peace of mind. Meditation is about clarity and living in an honest, straightforward relation to your world. Meditation does not just make a permanent dent on your cushion. It also makes a deep impact on the way you live your life.

Recent decades have seen a groundswell of research into the benefits of mindfulness meditation. Mindfulness's many benefits are now a part of general public knowledge and accepted scientific fact. Among these benefits are:

- deeper concentration and less tendency to distraction
- the ability to focus on the present moment
- an increase in nonjudgmental awareness
- the ability to see your emotions objectively
- letting go of outdated identities
- a general increase in positive emotions

Are you starting to see how this could benefit your life and your motivation? We will talk about these benefits in more depth later, and then look at some exercises for really taking advantage of them to increase your motivation, but first I want to describe the general practice of mindfulness meditation so that we have a better context for understanding how it has such transformative power for giving you the energy and enthusiasm you need on your road to achieving your goals and dreams.

How to practice mindfulness meditation

Practicing mindfulness meditation is quite simple and does not require a lot of preparation or training. Anyone can get into it. All you have to do is make a little time. *Learning how* to do the practice *is* the practice.

To begin with, set aside five to ten minutes of your day, every day. Find a quiet place to sit. Traditionally, you sit on a cushion or a mat, but you can sit on a chair if you like. You can even lie down. Whatever works for you.

If you are sitting, sit with your back straight. Your eyes can be open or closed; it's up to you. You may find that closing your eyes helps keep you from distraction, at least in the beginning.

The basic practice of sitting meditation is just to place your mind on the breath. *Mindfulness* in this context means being mindful of the breath, just following it as it moves in and out. When thoughts and sensations arise, you notice them and simply return your attention to the breath. It does not really matter what kind of thoughts or feelings come up. They could be boring thoughts about what you need to get from the store, or they could be mean, angry, happy, funny, creative, passionate—whatever.

Whatever comes up, just mentally label it *thinking* and return your attention to the breath. That's the nonjudgmental awareness we talked about earlier—whatever comes up, don't try to decide whether it's good or bad, don't accept or reject it. Just gently say to yourself, *Thinking*, and gently redirect your attention to the breath.

As you follow the breath in and out, you want to pay attention to the sensation of the breath—the feeling of the cool in-breath on your nostrils, and the warmth of the out-breath, the rise and fall of your lungs as you breathe in and out, whether the breath is long or short, shallow or deep, hard or gentle, and so on. In general, when meditating on the breath, you don't try to change the quality of the breath, but just let your lungs breathe however is most natural at any given time, and watch that.

Breathing is an effortless, autonomic function of the body, so we normally don't pay any attention to it. It just goes on in the background, all the time. In the practice of mindfulness, however, we don't take the breath for granted. Instead, we learn to appreciate the breath in its simplicity and variation. We develop a sense of wonder at something so simple and so necessary—taking in lungfuls of healthful, life-giving oxygen, which are delivered to the different organs of our body by the circulation of our blood. If we can learn to love and appreciate the simple fact of being alive, we can love ourselves.

When you begin meditating, it may seem that your discursive thoughts, the so-called "monkey mind," have only increased. Actually, nothing has increased; you just never noticed how active your mind is. Just stick with the practice of remaining mindful of the breath. Slowly, the speed of your thoughts will decrease. You will begin to notice and enjoy the vivid richness of the direct, sensory quality of your experience. This is the beginning of coming in touch with a quality of yourself that is fundamentally awake. It is the discovery of an innate source of goodness deep within your being.

Making friends with yourself

By breathing your awareness to the breath and learning to appreciate the simplicity of the present moment, you develop a sense of love for yourself that is not based on stories that you tell yourself, your wishes, likes and dislikes, who you tell yourself you want to be, negative thoughts, and so on. Instead, this newfound self-love is based on a direct, honest relationship to your own mind. This relationship is what has been called *making friends with yourself*.

The very act of meditation is an act of kindness to yourself. By setting aside time to rest and watch the breath, you are demonstrating a willingness and a commitment to sit with yourself quietly and gently. That is an act of compassion, a declaration of unconditional friendship to yourself and a willingness to get to know your own mind and heart more deeply.

It may sound strange to hear, but most of us do not really know ourselves that well. That's because we never take the time to get to know ourselves. So it's important to take that time, to slow down and rest. In this state of rest, we become more familiar with our own thoughts and feelings. Through the process of making friends with ourselves in meditation, we equip ourselves with self-love and self-compassion. Thus we can forgive ourselves when we make mistakes, or offer ourselves gentle encouragement and advice when we feel overwhelmed or anxious. This becomes a safeguard against the pessimism that attacks our motivation.

Deeper Concentration

It's easy to see how improving your concentration can increase your motivation to achieve your goals. In our daily lives, we're assailed from all sides by distractions and events vying for our attention. Meditation helps keep us on track by reducing the noise inside our heads. With more mindfulness, we will feel empowered to work towards our goals without going off track.

By bringing us into the present moment, mindfulness meditation helps induce a creative state of awareness psychologists call *flow*. Flow is full absorption in an activity with energetic focus and enjoyment. Research shows that mindfulness increases flow, focus, sharp thinking, self-control, and even the ability to meet deadlines.

Focus on the present moment

In increasing your motivation, it's often helpful to clarify what you want for the future. If you know your desired outcome, that positive vision of the future can give you the energy that spurs you along on your journey to success.

But it's just as easy to fall into the trap of imagining the possibility of failure, disaster, and worst-case scenarios, or succumbing to negative, discouraging memories from the past. When that happens, we feel burdened by negative emotions, our energy and drive diminish, and we lose our motivation.

Instead of causing us to dwell on the past or imagine the future, mindfulness brings our awareness into the present moment. With mindfulness, we cultivate an appreciation for the fullness of our living, breathing situation *right now*. This appreciation for the now lifts our spirits, increases our energy, and brings out a sense of courage within us that allows us to tackle the many challenges of life with cheerfulness and good humor. Living in the present moment, we feel encouraged and motivated in our lives; we sit on solid ground and are not easily knocked off our balance into discouragement and negativity.

Nonjudgmental awareness

For most of us, all sorts of thoughts come into our mind all the time. There is a constant mental chatter going, a running commentary on every aspect of ourselves and our lives.

Oh, Alicia's dress looks nice, I wonder where she bought it? I wish I looked as good in my clothes.

My boss is not going to be satisfied with my work this month, which will really hurt my chances of getting a raise.

I shouldn't have said that thing at the party last night, I really made a fool of myself.

And so on. We are always making stories and comments in our heads, judging ourselves, people, places, things, events, and so on as *good* or *bad*. When this negative commentary turns inward, we can find ourselves doubting our abilities and undermining our own efforts.

Mindfulness brings us in touch with a

nonjudgmental awareness, which is not concerned with deciding if things are good or bad, pleasurable or painful, desirable or undesirable. Whatever arises in our mind or outside in the world, we learn to accept it without judgment. In this way, meditation allows us to make friends with ourselves, fundamentally—to be kind and loving to ourselves.

In the context of motivation, nonjudgmental awareness comes to our aid because it keeps us from sinking into discouragement, pessimism, and self-doubt. Because we are making friends with ourselves through the practice of mindfulness, we do not critique and nay-say every aspect of our performance; instead, we learn to feel a natural, gentle encouragement that comes from within. Thus our self-confidence and positive motivation are buoyed by a tide of self-love and inner gentleness.

Emotional objectivity

Connected with the idea of nonjudgmental awareness is emotional objectivity. As human beings, we cannot just mechanically go through our life performing our functions like robots. We're emotional creatures with a rich, colorful inner life full of love and hate, anger, happiness, hope, fear, and so on.

But although emotions are part of the richness of our being, it is all too easy to get swept up in them and lose all sense of perspective. That makes it easy to get knocked off track. Since motivation is an emotional force, it too can get swept away by the current of strong feelings.

Mindfulness meditation allows us to abide in and maintain perspective about our emotions. That does not mean cutting ourselves off from emotional energy, like performing an amputation. What it does mean is increasing our sense of clarity, so that we can look at our emotions honestly, without getting hooked by them or rejecting them altogether.

That is an invaluable resource when we are working towards our goals. The emotional objectivity afforded by mindfulness gives us clarity about what we want and why we want it. It also allows us to keep some distance and perspective when powerful feelings come along that threaten to undo our hard work or blow us off course.

Moving past outmoded identities

One of the things that meditators notice about their minds is that, usually, when we are not being mindful, there is a constant stream of thoughts going on about this or that. These thoughts take the form of statements and judgments about ourselves and the world. Emotions color these thoughts, so that some of them are hopeful and some fearful, some passionate and some aggressive, some jealous, some compassionate and empathetic, some cold and calculating, some generous, and some selfish.

When you take a good look at these thoughts, you'll find that many or most of them use words like *I* or *me*. And a great number of those *I* and *me* thoughts repeat themselves again and again.

The thoughts come at such a rapid pace that they create the illusion of solidity and reality. If you've ever slowed down a film reel you'll know what I'm talking about. At its normal pace, a movie seems to be a continuous flow. If you slow the reel, the illusion is broken, and you see that what seemed like an unbroken continuity is actually made up of many individual frames.

We all have a sense of who we are, where we come from, what we stand for, what we will and will not do, what kind of person we are—a sense of *self-identity*. But this self-identity is much like the illusion created by a film reel. The *I*-thoughts in our mind come so fast that we never have the chance to step back and see the gaps in the picture they create.

Meditation gives us the chance to step back, slow down the film reel of our thoughts, and eye things at a distance. And what we find when we do that is that many of our ideas and thoughts about ourselves are limiting our personal growth and standing between us and our goals by constantly undermining our true desires.

If you find yourself resisting necessary change because "It's just not me," or being overly critical of yourself in a way that thwarts progress, it may be the case that your old identity is becoming an obstacle in your life. In this case, the practice of self-honesty through meditation can help loosen that tight grip on your old, out-of-date identity that is standing in the way of your self-actualization.

Increasing positive emotions

It goes without saying that no one ever gets very far on their path if they are overly negative, self-critical, and feeling down all the time. Even if we do manage to make some good progress, stress and so on leave us in danger of burning out. Negative emotions undermine our motivation and create doubts that stall us on our journey.

Fortunately, mindfulness is proven to increase positive emotions. This has been known for thousands of years, but recent research has corroborated that meditation increases happiness, empathy, emotional regulation, while reducing stress, anxiety, and depression. That's good news for you if you're trying to increase your motivation, because it means that your road to achieving your goals does not have to be a stressful one, and mindfulness will give you the resilience and equanimity you need to handle the emotional bumps in the road.

Bringing mindfulness into everyday life

Mindfulness that stays on the meditation cushion isn't going to bring much overall benefit to you. It might be nice to relax and take a break, but to really experience the power of mindfulness for improving your motivation, you have to take the lessons from your meditation practice and work them into everyday life.

One way to do this is by bringing mindful awareness into simple, everyday tasks. You could start by just being mindful when you're walking. Pay attention to the sensation as your foot touches the ground, the feeling in your legs as they move one after the other, the quality of your breathing as you walk—is it shallow, fast, or short?

You can bring mindfulness into simple activities like washing the dishes or brushing your teeth. Feel the temperature of the water and the slipperiness of the soap as you scrub plates. As you brush your teeth, pay attention to the sensation of the toothbrush as it glides over each individual tooth, the taste and smell of the toothpaste, the foamy later in your mouth.

Whatever activity you are doing, let yourself rest in the awareness of the sensory quality of your experience. Whatever you do is an embodied activity with a physical dimension, and being mindful of that is a very effective way to ground yourself and bring yourself into the present moment.

Once that becomes a habit, it is also incredibly beneficial to practice what's called *mindfulness of mind*. Be aware of what's happening in your mind as you walk, how when you see certain things you get distracted, how different events alter your mood, what kinds of thoughts and emotions come up. Remember, this is a process of getting to know yourself, so you don't have to judge what comes up in your mind—just pay attention to what's going on in there.

Exercise for this chapter

If you've never practiced meditation before, go ahead and try it out today. Set a time and arrange a quiet place where you will not be disturbed for five or ten minutes. Cross your legs, keep your back straight, and place your mind on the breath as we discussed earlier. Don't spend too long at this—you're just trying to build a familiarity with the practice, not win a mindfulness marathon. Give yourself some time to ease into the practice before you start sitting for longer sessions.

If you already have some experience with mindfulness meditation, that's great! Try to make it a daily practice. I find that morning is the best time for meditating; a morning session sets the right tone for the rest of the day. If you're already maintaining a consistent, daily practice, then all the better. Keep up the good work!

Notes:

Chapter Three
Mindful Motivation Techniques

So far we've covered the basics of mindfulness meditation, as well as how to work mindfulness into your daily life off the cushion. We've also talked about some of the benefits of mindfulness and how they can help increase your motivation and decrease the obstacles that get in your way.

Now I want to tell you about specific mindfulness techniques to boost motivation. These are meant as supplements to a daily meditation practice. A regular, consistent sitting meditation practice will create the right atmosphere of mindfulness in your life. It sets the mood. Within that atmosphere, we can also use targeted, specific techniques to improve our motivation.

The exercises that follow are meant to help you, but you might find that some are more suitable for you and some are not. Or it may be that some of them work better at some times, and others work better at other times. That's okay. This section is meant to help you start building a tool-kit of techniques that will boost your motivation. Out of this tool-kit, you can pick and choose your favorite tools, whichever ones are right for the job.

Doing in the Now

Consider what's involved in setting goals and working towards them. Dreams, goals, and ambitions come in all shapes and sizes, but let's consider a small one first.

Suppose you're dying to have a banana smoothie. This is a pretty simple and easy goal, and unless you're feeling super lazy, it won't be hard to work up the motivation to achieve it. Chances are, pretty soon you'll be enjoying that smoothie.

Why's that? Well, smoothies are easy to get, of course. They don't cost much and they are available in many places. But another reason you may not have considered is that the goal is not very intimidating. Because it's so easy to achieve, you won't come up against much internal resistance. You won't feel a sense of dread about the hardship, struggle, or boredom you'll have to go through to enjoy that smoothie that rewards your efforts.

Whatever your goal or vision might be, it's probably a much bigger deal than drinking a smoothie, not to mention some way off into the distant future, more or less. That means you're going to have to work hard for it. It also means there will be some irritation, boredom, and difficulty along the way.

That doesn't have to be a problem. In fact, it's a part of life. But when the tasks and work that lie ahead of us seem too big and intimidating, we dread the hard work it will take to complete them. That anxiety leads us to avoid what we need to do. It actually provides a strong *negative* motivation—to procrastinate or dream small.

That's where mindfulness comes in. Instead of trying to accomplish one giant goal, you can try to work on smaller goals instead, one after the other. Break it down so that you're working on just one simple thing at a time, and let yourself get absorbed into that task fully.

Remember how we talked earlier about *flow*? You'll recall that flow is when you get absorbed in what you're doing, and you're enjoying it and feeling energetic at the same time. When you're in flow, you're not dreading or worrying about anything. You're just *doing*.

Break down your goals into smaller pieces, and as you work on each piece, don't think too much about what you're doing—just *do*. Just get into the action of it, become one with it, and let yourself experience what you're doing mindfully.

Let's say your goal is to lose ten kilograms. How will you do that? Well, you can diet and exercise. Let's focus on exercise. You have to break that down into specific steps, also. So to start with, you could begin running two kilometers every day. And you have to begin with the first day.

On that first run, if you're constantly thinking about how you're going to lose that ten kg, and when will you fit into those old jeans again, etc., you'll start to feel discouraged pretty quickly. Instead of all that over-thinking, you can bring mindfulness on your run with you. Let yourself really feel the sensation of the running shoes slipping onto your feet, the laces tightening. Step outside—is the air warm or hot? Is it dry or muggy? Or maybe the air is cool and crisp with a winter chill, and feels sharp and cold in your lungs.

Then you get going. With each step as you run, your

foot hits the ground. You can feel the impact in your legs. As you pick up the pace, you can feel your heart rate going up. As you keep going, your limbs start to tire and your body wants to slow down. Because you're practicing mindfulness as you run, you don't just automatically start walking unconsciously; you are alert and in the moment, absorbed in what you're doing, enjoying it.

As you get absorbed in what you're doing with mindfulness, resting in a nonjudgmental awareness of all sensations and thoughts as they arise, there's no room for dread to come up. You're already doing it, and it's not so bad—in fact, it's kind of nice. It kind of feels good.

Mindfulness of Impermanence

When we have hard work ahead of us and our motivation is low, we sometimes *act* as if we had all the time in the world. So we procrastinate and do something else instead, something that is easy and offers an immediate reward. This may satisfy our desire for instant gratification--at least in the meantime—but in the long term, it will only get us stuck feeling regretful and dissatisfied.

We *know*, if we take a moment to reflect on it, that our time is limited. Mindfulness of impermanence is about taking that moment to reflect. When you find yourself procrastinating, distracted, or feeling to urge to blow off the work you know will bring you closer to your vision of the future, then stop and think to yourself:

> *Every moment, time is constantly passing me by. Each second ticks away, and seconds become minutes. Minutes become hours, and hours days. Time never stands still, so why act like I can put it on hold?*

> *I won't be the victim of my own inertia. I will be aware of the constant flow of time. Now is the only time to work towards achieving my dreams and goals.*

When it's time to start working on your goals, first take a minute to reflect and be mindful of the passage of time. Recall that time is limited. If you don't start doing it now, it will never get done. Get into the habit of renewing your motivation periodically by recalling the mindfulness of impermanence.

Envisioning the future

Everyone will tell you that to motivate yourself, you need to imagine your ideal future. And that's great. The vision of you accomplishing your goals can be an excellent motivator.

What many people won't tell you is that it also provides excellent motivation to imagine what would happen if you just let yourself go. What would your future be like if you gave yourself over to your worst tendencies? What would happen to your life if you let procrastination, inertia, boredom, time wasting, and bad habits take over?

It helps to think about the worst-case scenario because often we are not mindful of the real costs of counterproductive behavioral patterns. These patterns have a way of repeating themselves and turning into habits that are very difficult to change. In order to break them, we first have to understand *why* they are so harmful to us. Then, when they try to assert themselves again, we can summon the will-power to overcome them.

But don't spend too much of your time envisioning a future of doom and gloom. That could cause you to fall into anxiety and depression, which will definite *not* be good motivators. I suggest spending just fifteen to twenty minutes thinking about this worst case scenario one time. It can also help to spend that twenty minutes writing it down in a journal, then closing that journal and putting it away somewhere.

After you have imagined the *bad* future—and I do mean *right after*—you should spend some time envisioning your ideal future. Close your eyes and really build up a rich picture in your imagination. Fill it in with many details—sights, colors, sounds, smells, tastes.

This *your* vision of the future, and it should be strong and compelling.

It is important you don't skip over this second part, because simply imagining a negative future could ruin your mood and your motivation. You need a positive vision to counter the negative one, and then you will have a strong idea of the choices you face and the roads you can go down. You already know which one you want to travel.

If you are struggling with anxiety or depression now, or you have struggled with them in the past, this exercise may not be for you. You might consider passing on it. It's up to you.

It's worth repeating that these exercises should be practiced within the overall context of mental well-being that comes out of a strong mindfulness practice. Then, when negative thoughts and emotions come up, they won't "hook" you so powerfully. Not to mention a regular mindfulness practice is clinically proven to lower stress, depression, and anxiety, which will leave you feeling better and ready to take on life's challenges with gusto.

Eating a healthy diet

In order to keep you functioning at your optimal level, it's important that you eat a healthy, varied diet that gives you the proper nutrition you need.

You may be wondering what this section is doing on a book on mindfulness and motivation. After all, isn't mindfulness about being more aware, appreciating the moment, not getting distracted, and so on? What does all that have to do with healthy eating?

Actually, it has a lot to do with healthy eating. It is now well known that getting the proper nourishment for your body helps you improve and regulate your mood. That shouldn't be a surprise, because the body is the support for the mind. With a shaky and unhealthy support, your mind will also be shaky and unhealthy.

This is not the place to get into the details of planning and keeping a healthy diet. But there are abundant and excellent resources out there that will help you do just that. Remember, you don't have to go so overboard with eating healthy that it becomes your number one concern. In general, it's good to follow the advice *eat to live, don't live to eat. Simply remember to eat a natural, wholesome diet rich in fresh local fruits and vegetables.*

In addition to a healthy diet, you might want to take a few supplements that will improve your mental functioning. One of my favorites is *ashvagandha,* an ayurvedic medicine that research has shown regulates anxiety and stress hormones, increases your energy and mood, and gives you a number of cognitive boosts, such as improved concentration and memory. Do I need to mention that all of those things are important factors in keeping your motivation level high?

Again, you don't need to go overboard and take

every supplement known to humanity. Just find one or two that work well for you, to give you an extra push on your journey.

Breaking the chain reaction

Sometimes you're progressing towards your goals, keeping a pretty good pace. You're on a roll, when you suddenly hit a small obstacle. At that time, you might feel an urge to pack it in for the day, go check Facebook, take a walk, or do whatever.

I'm all for taking scheduled breaks. On a regular basis, you need to let yourself rest. Otherwise, you'll just wear yourself down and get burnout. But what happens when, after hitting a rough patch, you decide to take an unscheduled break, and that break is followed by another break, and another? Pretty soon you have an endless series of breaks, and you're left wondering what happened to your time and your motivation.

It's better not to go down that road to begin with. Fortunately, as you mature in your mindfulness practice, you will gain a certain distance from your thoughts, emotions, desires, and urges—a distance we earlier called *emotional objectivity*. The urge to take a detour or procrastinate won't catch you by surprise. You'll actually witness it coming up in your mind—and because you'll be a practiced meditator, you'll just let it be. No need to act on it.

Mindfulness meditation opens up a gap in the usual procedure of our minds. Normally, something happens. We see something, hear something, or think something. That provides the stimulus, which makes us feel one way or another. The many events we come into contact with all the time make us feel good, bad, or neutral. Based on that, we have an urge to act one way or another.

The next step is usually that we form a specific intention to act in a certain way, and then we just carry out the action. But with mindfulness, we can arrest the whole process at the urge. When we find ourselves wanting to act in one way or another, a gap just naturally opens up because of the mindfulness practice we've been doing. Within that gap, we can make a free and deliberate choice: take action, or just let it be. Which is the better choice will depend on the situation. But the point is that it's actually possible to break the usual chain reaction that compels us to certain behaviors and assert our own free will.

Notes:

Chapter Four
What to Do When Problems Come Up

I'd love to tell you that the journey to actualizing your dreams will be all smooth sailing and blue skies. But we all know that all sorts of problems, big and small, come up in life, and your journey will not always be a breeze. Anything worth doing in life is going run into obstacles and difficulties. So here are a few pointers about how to deal with them in a mindful way.

Mistakes

Everybody makes mistakes. They're an inevitable part of life, and we can learn from them. But sometimes we can be too harsh on ourselves for making mistakes, putting a lot of blame on ourselves and feeling guilty or ashamed. This can kill our energy and motivation: we put all that energy into blaming ourselves, and none is left over for actualizing our goals. Not only that, but we feel lousy and discouraged from our path.

Mindfulness is a big help here. Remember that nonjudgmental awareness I talked about earlier? It comes into play in an important way when we make mistakes. Instead of telling ourselves, *I really messed up, I'm such a jerk/fool/loser*, we can look calmly at the causes and conditions that went into the mistake. *A mistake occurred because of XYZ.* Then, since we know how the mistake happened, we can avoid making it again.

It doesn't matter if the mistake is big or small. It could be something as big as losing a friend over something you did or said, or something as small as not checking anything off your to-do list one day. Whatever the case, don't be too hard on yourself.

It bears repeating: Mindfulness meditation is a process of *making friends with yourself.* Do you jump on your friend's case every time he or she makes a mistake? No? Then there's no need to do it to yourself. Be kind to yourself and forgive yourself for the errors that you make. Then summon up the courage to continue on your path, avoiding the same mistakes in the future.

Disappointment and frustration

Disappointment and frustration are a familiar part of everyone's experience, and they are bound to come up. When they do, they will threaten to overturn your motivation. You may feel like just giving up.

That feeling of despair that makes you want to give up is just another strong emotion that arises in your mind, stays for awhile, then subsides again. Don't identify with the emotion and let it grip you.

Instead, think to yourself, *A feeling has come up*, and just let it be. Watch it, feel its texture, what kinds of thoughts come along with it, where the feeling occurs in the body—because, if you pay attention, you'll find that all emotions occur somewhere in the body. Looking closely at your frustration and disappointment, you'll find that the emotion is not some single overpowering force, but is made up of a number of parts. There's a part of it that consists of thoughts, a part that is a sensation felt in the body, a part that is a feeling-tone energy with a certain force and direction.

Don't try to suppress the feeling, but don't give into it, either. If you pay attention to it, mindfully, something remarkable will happen. The emotion will start to dissolve all by itself, without your having to do anything. It will release its energy, and you will be free to direct that energy to a positive purpose.

Stress

A big part of stress is a physiological response in the body that psychologists call "fight or flight" mode. Stress is basically a response to something that your body and brain experience as a threat. So your heart rate increases, your muscles tense up, your breathing accelerates, blood pressure goes up, your digestive system is inhibited.

None of this is a problem if you're staring down a predator in the jungle. In fact, it's a good thing, because it gets you ready to either fight for your life, or run away very fast. And, in the wilderness, you'll need to do one of those things if you hope to live.

But in our hectic modern lives, it's often the case that what our brain experiences as a threat does not go away. So we stay in fight-or-flight for days, months, years. We can't sleep properly, often we don't feel like eating, and we're generally just miserable. Eventually it takes a big toll on our health and can lead to a number of diseases.

Notes:

    The good news is that meditation just by itself is shown to reduce stress very effectively. In addition to that, however, there are a few things you can do to bring your stress levels down. The most important thing to do is find ways to rest. Even if you are very busy, take some *me* time to just relax.

    By "resting" I don't just mean sleeping, although that's important, too. I mean doing things that you find intrinsically enjoyable—that you don't have to force yourself to do, because you *want* to do them. That can be enjoying a tasty meal, talking a long walk in the afternoon, going for a swim, spending time with loved ones. Exercise is an excellent method for lowering stress, as is relaxing with friends and family.

The basic idea is that, since your brain thinks you are in danger, you need to do things that make the brain feel safe. You don't have to force your stress levels down. Just engage in some restful, enjoyable activity, and the stress will go down all by itself.

Doubt and fear

Maybe you have all kinds of doubts about yourself,

such as thoughts that you're not good enough, or smart, capable, or knowledgeable enough to achieve success. Or maybe you are fearful for the future, imagining all kinds of things that can go wrong.

Remember how we talked about *I*-thoughts and letting go of old identities? The self-doubts that come into your head again and again are an excellent example of *I*-thoughts that are holding you back from your goals. Look at these thoughts directly, but don't engage them with more thinking. Just watch them when they come up. Think to yourself, *A doubt is occurring*. Just label it *Thinking* and let it go.

Fear of things going wrong comes with imagining all kinds of bad scenarios. Yes, I know I told you to imagine a worst-case scenario earlier. That was just a one-time exercise for the purpose of clarifying your motivation. You definitely don't want to make a habit of it.

When you find your imagination wandering to the future and imagining scary scenarios, you know your mind has wandered from the present moment. In that case, gently guide your attention back to whatever you are doing. Don't feel guilty about losing your mindfulness, and don't judge yourself for your wandering mind. Just, again, label the fear *Thinking* and return to the task at hand.

In time you'll find that, whatever you are doing, you are more and more able to "keep your seat." That is, when strong feelings or unexpected events occur, they don't knock you off your balance, but you maintain your equilibrium and deal with things skillfully. But this takes time and practice. Until that day comes, don't get disheartened when you lose your seat; you can always catch yourself and find it again.

Working with low energy

It happens to the best of us. We run out of steam, or we never pick up any steam to begin with. Our mood can best be described as "blah," totally apathetic or maybe depressed. We just don't have any energy to be bothered with anything. Every task we need to do seems like such a demanding and awful chore.

It's not just a matter of this low-energy state sucking all the life out of your motivation. When your energy is low, you have very little confidence in yourself, and other people can sense it. They may avoid you, or ignore what you say, not take you seriously, and so on. Unconsciously, they may even blame you for mistakes that were not even your fault.

Even in meditation, you might slip into a state in which your energy is low and you are not particularly attentive or alert. It may feel like a fog has settled over you. You feel dull and sleepy. In that case, you can imagine that you are sitting on the peak of a mountain, with the bright harsh sun shining above you and the cold wind blowing against your skin. When you breathe in, imagine that a golden light fills your body. This method will restore alertness and energy to your mind when you're sitting.

Off the cushion, plenty of exercise and a healthy diet are important for keeping your energy levels up, as I mentioned above. Get up, go outside, try something new and exciting. If you can manage it, take a vacation and go on an adventure. Whatever you do, don't just sit around and stew in your own juices.

In some cases, however, a lack of energy is telling you something important. It may be that what you are trying to do, what you are trying to accomplish, is not something that you are truly passionate about. In that case, it's a case of intrinsic versus extrinsic motivation. You have no intrinsic motivation to accomplish your goals because, well, the goals didn't really come from *you*.

In such cases, there's nothing for it but to change

your life so that you're pursuing what you really value and are passionate about. This requires a lot of self-honesty and courage, but you will find all the inner resources you need through the practice of meditation. A strong mindfulness practice will give you clarity about what you really want and what you really value, as opposed to what you've been *told* you *should* want or value. It will act as a compass guiding you through life and telling you when you're not where you should be—and also, when you're moving in the right direction.

      We have covered the basics of what motivation is, as well as the definition of mindfulness and how to practice it. We've discussed the many benefits of mindfulness and how they can help you increase your motivation, as well as how to bring mindfulness off the cushion into your daily life. We've looked at a few techniques that will help you jump-start your motivation when it's down. Finally, we've talked about how to work with a number of problems that can arise and reduce your motivation if you let them—and how to not let them.

      You now have all the basic knowledge and tools you need to start practicing mindfulness to increase your motivation *today*. I hope this book itself has given you some inspiration and motivation to begin. I wish you many blessings and all the best on your journey. Good luck!

I wish you success, focus and unlimited motivation,

Until next time,

James Adler

PS. Can I ask you a quick favor? If you enjoyed this book, please take the time to share your thoughts and post a review online. It would be greatly appreciated!

Your honest review is a great way to let others know of the benefits you've got from mindfulness based motivational strategies. This will not only help others reach their goals, but it is incredibly rewarding for me to know how much my work has benefited others! This way you can help empower others in the way Mindfulness has empowered you…

You can also email me at:
elenajamesbooks@gmail.com

More books available at:

www.YourWellnessBooks.com

www.ingramcontent.com/pod-product-compliance
Lightning Source LLC
Chambersburg PA
CBHW042121100526
44587CB00025B/4149